At Home in This World

FOR
MELANIE Jia Lu —
BEST WISHES!
Jean

EMK

At *Home* in this *World*

住家庭愛 . . . a China adoption story

by Jean MacLeod
illustrations by Qin Su

At Home in This World, a China adoption story
text © 2003 Jean MacLeod
illustrations © 2003 Qin Su

ISBN 0-9726244-1-4

Library of Congress Control Number: 2003107585
Cataloging-in-Publication data available on request

First Edition   September, 2003

Printed in China
printed on acid free paper, binding reinforced
Set in Goudy, illustrations are watercolor

Published by EMK Press, a division of EMK Group, LLC
16 Mt Bethel Road, #219
Warren, NJ 07059
www.emkpress.com

EMK Press is dedicated to publishing projects that directly benefit the children who remain in institutions throughout the world. The Author's royalties and a portion of the publishing proceeds will be contributed to charities that work to improve the lives of these children, who wait and wish for families of their own. Proceeds from this book will benefit the following charities:

Families with Children from China National Appeal
The FCC National Appeal directly helps children in China's orphanages by funding surgeries, providing for foster care, paying school fees, building playgrounds and supplying institutions with life-saving heaters, washers and air conditioners. FCC sends 100% of each dollar it receives to China. www.fwcc.org

Our Chinese Daughters Foundation
OCDF is a non-profit foundation that supports families with children adopted from China. OCDF provides: Travel Programs and Chinese Cultural Programs in China for families with adopted children, the OCDF Newsletter, and the China for Children Magazine. Grants are awarded to local and regional support groups and adoption agencies to assist with workshops/seminars and Chinese cultural programs for all adoptive families. www.ocdf.org

An Invitation

I am the mother of three girls, two of whom were adopted as babies from China. I mourned the lost first months that my adopted daughters spent across the ocean without me, and I was determined that they would be surrounded by love and emotional comfort once they were in my arms. As they grew older, I told them stories of a caring birthmother who lovingly relinquished them to good parents and a better life. I edited hours of video footage so they could see the first joyous moments of becoming a part of our family, and I spent days putting together a baby-book heavy on happy adoption-day photographs. I gave them everything I thought they would need from me to feel wanted and cherished, when what they really needed from me was… the truth.

The relentlessly positive spin I chose to put on my girls pre-adoption birth story was confusing to my daughters, who recognized buried feelings that didn't always parallel mine. Psychologist Doris Landry helped me to realize that addressing and legitimizing these feelings would both strengthen my children, and connect them to me with a powerfully intimate mother-daughter bond.

My adopted children had lives, and families, before me."You mean it's okay to love two Moms?" my seven year old from China once asked me incredulously. "Oh yes" I told her. "Your birthmother will always be in our hearts." My daughter's face was a mix of relief, amazement and joy. Love only multiplies, I could have added, and love based on truth is indestructible.

I invite you and your family into this book of love and loss–the bittersweet feelings that define adoption. Hoping to celebrate our children's strength and resiliency, I have created this "forever" story for all of us adoptive parents, and for the brave baby hearts in all our forever children.

Jean MacLeod

For my daughters, my world
Molly, Lily and Hanna

A special thank you to the talented people who made
this book a reality: Brian Boyd, Carrie Kitze, Doris Landry,
Jane Liedtke and Michael Su

Jean MacLeod

The Chinese characters on the cover
represent something I wish
for all children in this world.

 住家 Home

家庭 Family

愛 Love

At *Home* *in this* *World*

住家庭愛

... a China adoption story

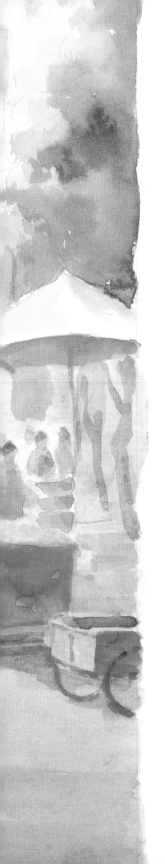

I am nine years old and someone a lot like you. Part of my life has been like a puzzle needing pieces, but I am understanding more about myself and my life everyday. This is my story...

I was born in China.

When I was a baby, my birthparents placed me in a busy spot in a big city. They left me there so I would be quickly found.

I don't remember my birthparents, but I will always remember the feeling of being alone.

Sometimes I try to make sense out of why my birthparents would leave me. My mom has explained that in China, most people are only allowed to have one child—or sometimes two if the first child is a girl.

Many Chinese parents really believe they must have a son to support them when they are old and not able to work. I might have been born a second daughter and my birthparents might have felt they needed a boy. Or maybe my birthmother was sick or disabled, and had no one to help her with a little baby.

I know that my birthparents must have had a sad reason of their own not to keep me, and I know it wasn't my fault—all babies are made to be loved.

I understand all of these things in my head, but it is so much harder to understand in my heart.

I think about my birthmother.

I don't know her, and yet I do because she is part of me. I know I was connected to my birthmother before I was born, while she carried me inside her. I learned how my birthmother moved, what foods she liked and how her voice sounded.

I sometimes wonder if I look like her.

My birthparents gave me my black hair and almond-shaped eyes and my long, piano-playing fingers. Maybe I am smart and graceful and good at music because they are too.

They will always be a piece of who I am.

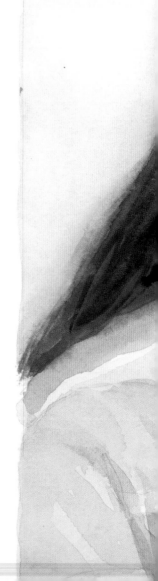

When I was found in China I was taken
to a police station and then to my
orphanage.

I was cared for by the Ayis, who fed me
and washed me and bundled me in many
layers to keep me warm. There were so
many babies that it was hard for the Ayis
to hug and hold and play with all of us
the way a parent would, and I know that I
cried.

When I imagine my story it's hard to
believe it ever happened to me. I don't
like to think about it much.

After a little while I was placed in a temporary home with a foster family.

Their house was in a small farming village near the orphanage. They didn't have much of anything, but they shared what they had with me-– and they gave me lots of attention!

I was carried on the back of my foster mother as she worked outside in the garden, and I learned about my world. I learned the smells, and I learned about noodles and what my favorite people looked like.

I learned how to smile.

One day my foster mother dressed me carefully. She put on my split pants and long-sleeved shirt and yellow socks, and over it all she placed a pretty pink party dress that was a little too big.

My foster mother told me that I was going to be adopted by strangers from far away, but that I would be very happy in my new family.

Now, when I watch my adoption video, I can tell that I was a very confused little baby. My mom and dad look excited at meeting me, but I didn't know who they were and I look a lot more worried than happy.

When the orphanage Director handed me to my new parents in the hallway of a hotel in China, my whole world changed.

I had a permanent family who promised the orphanage Director and the Chinese government that they would love and take care of me for always.

It was all a blur after that.

I had to get used to a new mama and baba, but I see in my pictures how they cuddled me and made me giggle. I think I must have felt they were very nice, very special people.

My mom carried me all over China in
a sling, close against her. My dad played
peek-a-boo with me and fed me rice
congee out of a coffee mug in our
hotel room.

We were learning how to be a family,
and I liked how that felt.

My parents brought me to their house, which was a long airplane ride away from where I was born. The smells were funny, the food was different, and the sounds were strange. It was another big change to get used to and I wondered what had happened to everything I had known! I think I knew that my mom and dad loved me, but it took me awhile to understand that they wouldn't disappear one day, too.

I couldn't always escape the dreams of being lost that would come after I fell asleep at night.

Sometimes my mom would hold me in the dark and rock me and sing. Her voice made me feel safe and warm– the way I felt when my dad held me to his shoulder and rubbed my back. My dreams aren't about being lost anymore, they are the usual jumble of crazy stuff that sleeping kids think about at night.

I don't have to be afraid… I'm home.

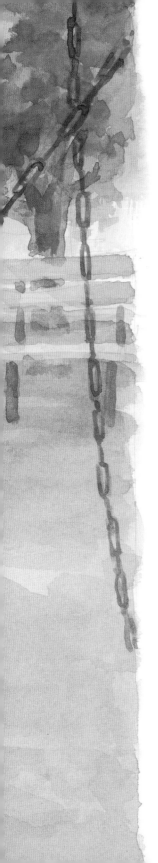

When I was a very little girl, my mom
explained to me what adoption meant.

I remember wishing that I had grown
inside my mom and that she looked
Chinese, like me.

Most of the time I didn't think about
being adopted at all.

I went to preschool and played with kids
at the park and just knew that Mama and
Daddy would always be my parents.

I'm not a little girl anymore; I play the piano and take ballet lessons and I ride my bike to school. I still like noodles, but my favorite food is strawberry ice cream. I have a cat and a little sister and two best friends.

Sometimes my friends will ask me questions about things I can't answer: I don't remember anything clearly about my first year on the other side of the ocean—all I have are memories of many different feelings, and sometimes what I feel I can't explain.

My mom and dad seem to know when I need to talk, even when I don't want to! They let me be exactly the way that I feel inside, and help me to understand that I'm not alone. There are lots of girls like me, and boys, who were adopted from China. Sometimes I get together with a group of these kids and it feels good to be the same as everyone else.

I still wonder about my life in China.

I love my parents very much and I
wouldn't want any other family, but
I think I will always miss knowing the
parents that weren't mine to keep.

My mom says that I am a brave kid
and that my life has been an amazing
adventure—that I have experienced
enormous changes, and I have survived
them all. I like to think about it that way;
it helps me bring both my sides together.

I was born in China and now I'm from
here, and my before and after is all part
of who I am: one girl from two places
who is growing up to be at home in this
big, wide world.

What is Your Story?

How does the girl in this book know so much about her life in China?

When she was adopted, her mom and dad were given very little information about her early life. With the help of her parents she gathered the tiny clues that gave her a history, and created her story with all she knew and what she guessed was probable.

You can re-create your history too, and piece together the puzzle of what life was like for you when you were small. It's not exactly the same as knowing all the facts, but it will give you more understanding of who you are and where you came from.

For some kids, the information that they have about their time in China is sad, or painful to talk about. What happened to you as a baby or child in China was out of your control, but your life story belongs to you, and you get to choose your future. You can learn about the tough early circumstances that you might have experienced, and better understand how they've shaped you to be the amazing kid that you are today.

What kind of clues can you look for? Start at home, by asking your mom or dad how you behaved the first year after you were adopted. What were your reactions to new situations? Were you anxious and easily frightened, or did you meet the world with a happy smile? Your behavior as a small child is one key to how you were cared for in China. It is also a look back to the personality that you inherited from your birthparents. Are you quiet or lively? Good at math or at reading? These are clues to what your birthparents might be like, too.

Ask your parents to help you search the Internet to find out about the city or place you spent your first months. What was the weather like on the day you were born? On the day you were found? How did the officials guess or know how old you were? Were you healthy and well-fed, or perhaps sick and in need of medical care?

Look at yourself in your referral photograph, and the pictures and videos of your first days with your new mom and dad. What do you think that little baby (or toddler or child) was thinking?

Where were you found? Many babies are left in public places like train stations, near government buildings or even in restrooms. Your birthparents probably looked for a place that was safe and maybe even protected from the weather. Very public places, or specially chosen places, increased the chance that you would be found quickly and taken care of.

Some babies form close relationships with the caretakers at their orphanage, and some become part of a foster family. All babies react to fear and loss- this is one important way to "know" that you probably missed your birthmother, and perhaps even another caretaker who was special to you, like an Ayi or a foster mother.

Contacting your adoption agency and asking them to help you get any additional information from your orphanage file may be helpful. Someday when you are ready, visiting your orphanage and "hometown" in China may give you another personal perspective about the world you came from, and the people who cared for you.

Clues are everywhere! Your reactions, other people's reactions to you, the clothes you were wearing, the foods you liked— think about the facts that you and your parents have about you as a baby or small child in China and at home, and what each of those facts really mean. Putting together your own, individual history with bits of details will eventually give you a bigger, clearer picture of yourself. Everyone has a life story, and with a little detective work you will be certain that no one has a life story as remarkable, as interesting or as extraordinary as your own.

Jean MacLeod

~~~~~~~~~~

Other resources:

Visit our website **www.emkpress.com** for an age specific reading list. You will also find a user guide for parents that talks about the core issues of adoption. As our children mature, their understanding and ideas of adoption change. This guide will help parents understand the building blocks to help our children and ourselves on this lifelong journey.